THE WHITE HOUSE HAS BEEN THE HOME
AND OFFICE TO EVERY PRESIDENT OF THE
UNITED STATES SINCE JOHN ADAMS.

6 JOHN QUINCY ADAMS
1825–29

7 ANDREW JACKSON
1829–37

8 MARTIN VAN BUREN
1837–41

9 WILLIAM HENRY HARRISON
1841

JOHN TYLER
1841–45

16 ABRAHAM LINCOLN
1861–65

17 ANDREW JOHNSON
1865–69

18 ULYSSES S. GRANT
1869–77

19 RUTHERFORD B. HAYES
1877–81

20 JAMES A. GARFIELD
1881

27 WILLIAM HOWARD TAFT
1909–13

28 WOODROW WILSON
1913–21

34 DWIGHT D. EISENHOWER
1953–61

35 JOHN F. KENNEDY
1961–63

41 GEORGE H. W. BUSH
1989–93

42 WILLIAM J. CLINTON
1993–2001

43 GEORGE W. BUSH
2001–09

44 BARACK OBAMA
2009–17

45 DONALD J. TRUMP
2017–

Introduction

The White House is the home and office of the President of the United States. It is a big place full of special rooms, beautiful things, and hard-working people who do important jobs. It takes every letter of the alphabet to tell all the stories found here!

Rocco Smirne is five years old. He has found every letter here from A—for *Air Force One* to Z—for Zip Code! Rocco's favorite picture is of *Marine One*, the helicopter drawn for the letter H. Rocco and his mother created this book to share a White House story for all twenty-six letters of the alphabet with you. They will take you to see the Marine Band, the Queens' Bedroom, the Oval Office, rooms that are all red, blue, and green, and more. I hope you will have fun on your tour!

Stewart D. McLaurin
President, White House Historical Association

A White House Alphabet

Illustrated by **John Hutton** • Text by **Arioth Harrison Smirne** with **Rocco Smirne**

Let's visit the White House! Every letter of the alphabet is found here!

THE WHITE HOUSE *HISTORICAL ASSOCIATION*

A is for *Air Force One*, a special airplane that takes the president to meetings around the world.

 is for **Blue Room**, a fancy room all in blue and gold where the president entertains guests. The Christmas Tree is often placed here in the middle of the room!

 is for **Commander in Chief**, another name for the president of the United States!

D is for **Diplomatic Reception Room**, where the president greets leaders of other countries.

E is for **East Room**, the largest room in the White House. Grand parties and special events happen here.

 is for First Ladies. They make people feel at home at the White House and work hard to help make the world a better place.

 is for **Green Room**, a special room with green walls, and green curtains, and green furniture! People often enjoy tea and cake in this room.

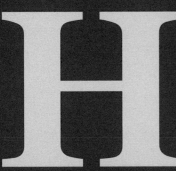 is for **Helicopter**. A special helicopter called *Marine One* picks up the president right from his backyard at the White House, to travel to meetings in many places.

I

is for **Inauguration**, the ceremony that marks the beginning of each presidential term when the president takes the Oath of Office. It takes place every four years on January 20.

J is for **Jackson Magnolia**, one of two old trees with big white flowers that grow just outside the back door of the White House. The tree is named for President Andrew Jackson.

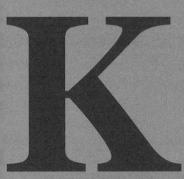

K is for the **Kitchen Garden** in the backyard of the White House. It is where healthy vegetables are grown for the president's table.

L is for **Lincoln Bedroom**, where the Lincoln Bed and other furniture that belonged to President Abraham Lincoln many years ago are still used today.

 is for **Marine Band**, which is also called the "The President's Own." The band performs grand music for the president and for White House events.

 is for **North Portico**, the front porch built with tall stone columns over the front door of the White House. Sometimes, the president's car parks right under the portico!

O

is for **Oval Office**, where the president works.

P

is for the **Portraits** of presidents that hang here!

Q is for **Queens' Bedroom**, a guest room where royalty from many countries have slept on visits to the White House.

R is for **Red Room**, which is decorated with red curtains, red walls, and red furniture.

S is for **State Dining Room**, a room that is used for fancy dinners, where the chef serves the best food.

T is for **Truman Balcony**, an upstairs balcony added to the South Portico by President Harry S. Truman. The president has a good view of Washington from here.

U

is for **United States Secret Service** officers who work hard to protect the president every day.

 is for **Vermeil**, which means silver dipped in gold! There are many vermeil bowls, plates, and other objects displayed in the Vermeil Room.

W

is for **West Wing**, where the president works. Many people with important White House jobs have offices here too.

 is for **X-Ray** machines that are used to check everything visitors bring into the White House in order to keep everyone safe.

Y is for **Yellow Oval Room**, which has yellow walls and has been used as the family library and formal sitting room.

is for Zip Code. If you write a letter to the president or first lady at 1600 Pennsylvania Avenue, be sure to add the zip code, 20500!

About the Authors

Arioth Harrison Smirne is the director of special events at the White House Historical Association. She holds a degree in English Literature from the University of Virginia. She lives in Virginia with her co-author and son, Rocco, husband, and youngest son, Luca.

About the Illustrator

John Hutton is a professor of art history at Salem College, where he has taught since 1990 and is the author of *How to Draw the Presidents.* He lives with his family in Winston-Salem, North Carolina.

Vice President of Publishing and Executive Editor: Marcia Mallet Anderson; Editorial and Production Director: Lauren McGwin; Senior Editorial and Production Manager: Kristen Hunter Mason; Editorial and Production Manager: Elyse Werling; Editorial Assistant: Rebecca Durgin; Consulting Editor: Ann Hofstra Grogg

Original drawings by John Hutton are dedicated by the artist to Vievey, Milo, and Bode. Copyright © 2020 by the White House Historical Association

10 9 8 7 6 5 4 3 2 1   Library of Congress Control Number: 2020936888   ISBN 978-1-950273-08-9   Printed in Italy